BURPS, SCABS and SMELLS

by Anita Ganeri

illustrated by Tony Trimmer

OXFORD
UNIVERSITY PRESS
AUSTRALIA & NEW ZEALAND

OXFORD
UNIVERSITY PRESS

Oxford University Press is a department of the University of Oxford.
It furthers the University's objective of excellence in research,
scholarship, and education by publishing worldwide. Oxford is a registered
trademark of Oxford University Press in the UK and in certain other countries.

Published in Australia by
Oxford University Press
Level 8, 737 Bourke Street, Docklands, Victoria 3008, Australia

First published 2014
This edition 2019
Reprinted 2020, 2021

ISBN 9780190318031

Series Editor: Nikki Gamble
Illustrations by Tony Trimmer
Designed by Oxford University Press in collaboration with Fiona Lee, Pounce Creative
Printed in China by Leo Paper Products Ltd

Contents

Is It OK to Pick a Scab?

Hi Dr Sicknote,

I've got a big scab on my knee. Is it OK to pick it?

Hello Emily!

I wouldn't, if I were you. Your scab's really useful.

It works like a bandage, covering your cut until it heals. Here's what happens …

1. When you cut yourself, special **blood cells** stick together. This is called a clot.

Your scab will fall off when it's ready – probably in a week or two.

If you pick your scab, the cut will take longer to heal and you could end up with a scar.

SO LEAVE IT ALONE!

sick note

Scabs are amazing. They stick the cut back together and keep nasty **germs** out.

2. The clot plugs the cut to stop it bleeding.

3. After the bleeding stops, the clot becomes dry and crusty. Now it's a scab.

Why Are Boogers Green?

Hi Dr Sicknote,

Why are my boogers green when I've got a cold?

Hello Dinesh!

This question really gets up my nose.

Boogers are made inside your nose from slimy stuff called **mucus**. Mucus traps dirt and germs and stops them reaching your lungs.

nose

mucus

Most of the time, mucus is clear. But it can turn green if you've got a cold. This is because it's full of blood cells that have come to fight and kill the germs. These cells have a green colour, which

TURNS YOUR BOOGERS GREEN!

Sick note
Your boogers are important. They're a sign that your nose is working properly. Remember, everyone has them!

What Makes Me Burp?

Hi Dr Sicknote,

Why do fizzy drinks always make me burp?

Hello Malia!

Fizzy drinks are full of gas – that's what makes them fizzy! When you swallow your drink, it goes down your **oesophagus** (*say* uh-sof-uh-gus) into your stomach. Some of the gas gets forced back up. It bursts out of your mouth as a burp.

The same thing can happen if you scoff your food too quickly. Burping is normal and natural. (Tell your parents I said so!) But it's always polite to say "Excuse me", or cover your mouth with your hand.

oesophagus

stomach

sick note

The loudest burp on record was noisier than a motorbike – and almost as loud as a chainsaw!

9

Why Do Farts Smell?

Hi Dr Sicknote,

Why are my sister's farts so smelly?

Hello Seth!

Are you *sure* it's your sister? I usually blame the dog.

Farts work a bit like burps. When you swallow your food, you also gulp down gassy air. As your body gets busy **digesting** your food, it makes more gas.

All that gas has to go somewhere – some of it comes out of your bottom!

Some farts are loud and don't smell. Others are silent, but super-stinky! That's because they're loaded with really smelly gases. Most people fart around 14 times a day – including your sister!

Sick note
Small insects such as termites and cockroaches fart more than any other creature – even more than dogs!

Food breaks down here (stomach).

Gas travels through here (large intestine).

Fart comes out here (anus).

Why Do I Have Wax in My Ears?

Hi Dr Sicknote,

Mum says I've got wax in my ears. What's it doing there?

Hello Sophia!

You do have wax in your ears – ear wax! Ear wax is squishy yellow stuff that keeps the insides of your ears clean. It traps harmful dust, dirt and germs, and stops your ears getting dry and itchy.

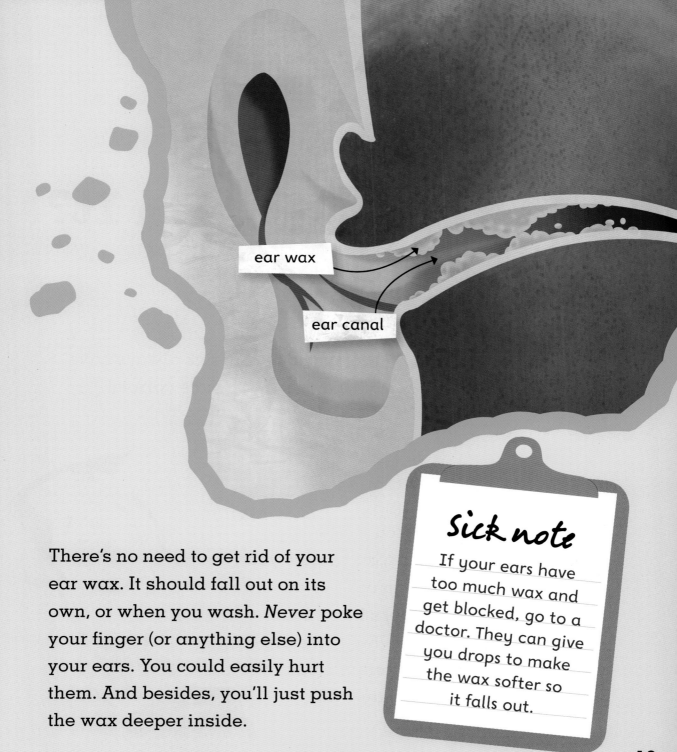

ear wax

ear canal

There's no need to get rid of your ear wax. It should fall out on its own, or when you wash. *Never poke your finger (or anything else) into your ears.* You could easily hurt them. And besides, you'll just push the wax deeper inside.

Sick note

If your ears have too much wax and get blocked, go to a doctor. They can give you drops to make the wax softer so it falls out.

Why Does Sick Have Carrots in It?

Hi Dr Sicknote,

Why does my sick always have carrots in it? I *hate* carrots!

Hello Sebastian!

It's strange, isn't it? You get that funny feeling in your tummy, and before you know it, you've thrown up your dinner. And **vomit** *always* looks like it's full of chopped-up carrots. But these are actually bits of all different foods that have been mixed up with your stomach juices.

14

3. The food comes out of the mouth as vomit.

2. This causes food to travel back up the oesophagus.

You see, throwing up is your body's way of getting rid of something nasty. Your stomach muscles squeeze until they've pushed your half-eaten food back up your throat and out of your mouth.

Sometimes you throw up because of germs in your tummy. Sometimes it's because you've eaten too fast or the food was off.

Start here.

1. The stomach muscles squeeze, pushing food upwards.

15

Why Am I Covered in Spots?

Hi Dr Sicknote,

Help! I'm covered in spots! What's wrong with me?

Hello Lien!

Have you got a runny nose and a cough, too? If so, you've probably got chickenpox.

Some people only get a few spots when they have chickenpox. Others get spots all over – even in their mouth and ears!

1. Spots start to appear on the skin.

After a few days, your spots will go crusty. They will probably itch *a lot*. I know it's hard, but try not to scratch them. If you do, germs might get in, or the spots might leave a scar.

2. After a while, the spots form blisters.

Chickenpox is easy to spread, too, so you should stay away from school until the scabs fall off. (See, it's not all bad news!)

Sick note

Nobody is sure how chickenpox got its name. It might be because the spots look like you've been pecked by a chicken!

3. Finally, the blisters dry up and get crusty.

How Can You Stop Hiccups?

HIC!

CUP!

HIC!

CUP!

Hi Dr Sicknote,

I've – *hic!* – got hiccups. How – *cup!* – can I make them – *hic!* – stop?

Hello Isaac!

Sometimes a fright helps.

BOO!

Did that work? If not, try drinking water from the wrong side of a glass, or hold your breath and count to ten.

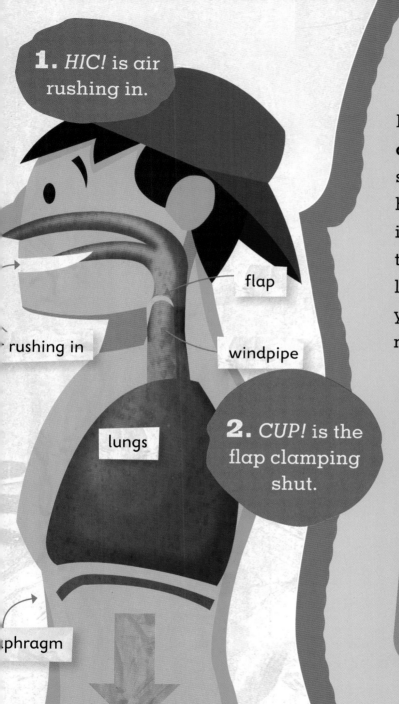

1. *HIC!* is air rushing in.

flap

rushing in

windpipe

lungs

2. *CUP!* is the flap clamping shut.

...phragm

Hiccups happen when your **diaphragm** (*say* dy-uh-fram) suddenly pulls down really hard, forcing you to suck in lots of air. To stop all that air rushing into your lungs, a flap at the top of your windpipe snaps shut, making a hiccuping sound!

Sick note

A man called Charles Osborne had the longest attack of hiccups ever recorded. His hiccups lasted for 68 years!

Why Do I Keep Yawning?

Hi Dr Sicknote,

Why do I always yawn as soon as I wake up?

Hello Kiera!

That's a good question! Nobody knows for sure, but there are lots of ideas.

Some people think that yawning is a way of helping your body wake up. When you yawn, you take in a big gulp of air. It's like a big stretch – for your lungs!

yawn

air

lungs getting bigger as they fill with air

One thing's for sure — yawning is **contagious**. If you see someone yawning, I bet you start yawning, too. You just can't help it. Sometimes just *thinking* about yawning can set you off!

Sick note

Everybody yawns — even babies in their mothers' tummies! Most people yawn around 240 000 times in their life. Each yawn lasts around six seconds.

Do Geese Get Goosebumps?

Hi Dr Sicknote,

When I'm c-c-cold, I always get goosebumps.

Do g-g-geese get them, too?

Hello Jerome!

No, they don't, because they don't have furry or hairy skin! They have feathers.

Your hairs stand on end because they're trying to keep you warm. This doesn't work very well, though, because you're not hairy enough!

Goosebumps were more useful long ago, when humans were much hairier.

sick note

Goosebumps got their name because they make your skin look like the knobbly skin of a goose that has been plucked for cooking. Yikes!

Here's how goosebumps happen:

1. When you get cold, the hairs on your body try to stand on end.

2. Each hair is attached to a tiny muscle that pulls it up.

3. The muscle also pulls up a tiny bump of skin, which we call a goosebump.

Glossary

blood cells: tiny parts that are in your blood

contagious: easily passed to other people

diaphragm: a flat muscle in your chest, underneath your lungs

digesting: breaking down your food into tiny pieces that can be used to help your body work

germs: tiny living things that can cause you to get sick

mucus: slippery material that lines your nose, lungs and stomach

oesophagus: the tube that carries food from your mouth to your stomach

vomit: food that has come back up from the stomach to the mouth

Index